SCIENCE EXPLORER

JUNIOR

JUNIOR SCIENTISTS

Experiment with Soil

by Vicky Franchino

CHERRY LAKE PUBLISHING · ANN ARBOR, MICHIGAN

NOTE TO PARENTS AND TEACHERS: Please review the instructions for these experiments before your children do them. Be sure to help them with any experiments you do not think they can safely conduct on their own.

NOTE TO KIDS: Be sure to ask an adult for help with these experiments. Always put your safety first!

CHERRY
LAKE
Publishing

Published in the United States of America by Cherry Lake Publishing
Ann Arbor, Michigan
www.cherrylakepublishing.com

Content Editor: Robert Wolffe, EdD, Professor of Teacher Education,
Bradley University, Peoria, Illinois
Reading Adviser: Cecilia Minden-Cupp, PhD, Literacy Consultant

Design and Illustration: The Design Lab

Photo Credits: Page 10, ©f. AnRo brook/Shutterstock, Inc.; page 15,
©iStockphoto.com/LUGO; page 16, ©iStockphoto.com/bobbieo; page
21, ©ollirg/Shutterstock, Inc.; page 22, ©iStockphoto.com/alicescully;
page 29, ©iStockphoto.com/JHLloyd

Library of Congress Cataloging-in-Publication Data
Franchino, Vicky.
  Junior scientists. Experiment with soil / by Vicky Franchino.
    p. cm.–(Science explorer junior)
  Includes bibliographical references and index.
  ISBN-13: 978-1-60279-837-3 (lib. bdg.)
  ISBN-10: 1-60279-837-0 (lib. bdg.)
  1. Soils—Experiments—Juvenile literature. I. Title. II. Title:
Experiment with soil. III. Series.
  S591.3.F729 2010
  631.4078–dc22   2009048820

Portions of the text have previously appeared in *Super Cool Science
Experiments: Soil* published by Cherry Lake Publishing.

Cherry Lake Publishing would like to acknowledge the work
of The Partnership for 21st Century Skills. Please visit
www.21stcenturyskills.org for more information.

Printed in the United States of America
Corporate Graphics Inc.
July 2010
CLFA07

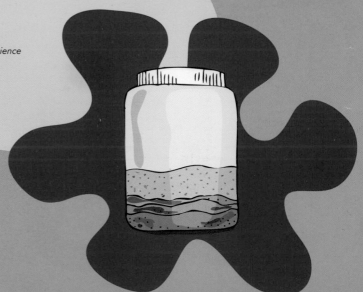

TABLE OF CONTENTS

Let's Experiment!

Experiments are fun!

Have you ever done a science **experiment**? They can be a lot of fun! You can use experiments to learn about almost anything.

This book will help you learn how to think like a scientist. Scientists have a special way of learning new things. Some people call it the Scientific Method. This is how it often works:

- Scientists notice things. They **observe** the world around them. They ask questions about things they see, hear, taste, touch, or smell. They come up with problems they would like to solve.

A scientist guesses what the answer to his question is.

- They gather information. They use what they already know to guess the answers to their questions. This kind of guess is called a **hypothesis**.

- Then they test their ideas. They perform experiments or build models. They watch and write down what happens. They learn from each new test.

Scientists record what happens during their experiments.

- They think about what they learned and reach a **conclusion**. This means they come up with an answer to their question. Sometimes they **conclude** that they need to do more experiments!

Conclusion: I need to do another experiment!

When a scientist figures out the answer to his question, he has reached a conclusion.

We will use the scientific method to learn more about soil. Soil is an important part of our world. Have you ever wondered what soil is made of? We can answer this question and others by doing experiments. Each experiment will teach us something new about soil. Are you ready to be a scientist?

A FEW WORDS ABOUT THE SOIL YOU'LL USE FOR THESE EXPERIMENTS:

Use soil that you dig up from your backyard or school. Ask your parents or teacher first! Don't use a bag of potting soil from a gardening center. Don't use soil that contains too much sand or clay, either. Are you doing these experiments in a classroom? Do you need a lot of soil? Try these places:

- Certain departments at a local college or university
- A local 4-H program
- Your local extension office. This government program does research related to agriculture. Agriculture is the study of farming. Find out if there's an office near you. Visit www.csrees.usda.gov/Extension/.

What Is Soil Made Of?

What do you see in the soil?

Soil is all around us. Have you ever wondered what is in soil?

Take a close look at some soil. You'll probably see many colors and **textures**. Why does soil look this way? Is it made up of many things or just one thing? We can find out by doing an experiment. First, let's choose a hypothesis:

1. Soil is made up of many different things.
2. Soil is made up of only one thing.

Let's get started!

Write down your hypothesis.

Hypothesis: Soil is made up of many different things.

Here's what you'll need:

- 1 cup of soil
- 1 glass jar with a lid. The jar should be big enough to hold 3 cups of water.
- 1 cup of water

Collect your materials.

Shake the jar until the water and soil are mixed well.

Instructions:

1. Place the soil in the jar. Add the water. Screw the lid on tightly. Shake the jar until the water and soil are mixed well.

2. Put the jar on a counter. Let the mixture settle overnight.

3. Observe the mixture the next day. Be sure to write down everything you see.

Do you see different layers in your jar?

Conclusion:

The mixture probably looks different now. Do you see layers in the jar? What makes up the different layers?

There are usually 3 main things in soil. They are sand, **silt**, and clay. Most soils have all 3 materials. Different soil might have more of one thing and less of another. Soil often has stones and bits of rotting plants, too.

Look at your layers of soil and water. Sand is the heaviest type of soil. Silt is lighter. Clay is the lightest. Which layer in your jar is sand? Which is silt? Which is clay? Does the soil have all 3 parts? Does it have more sand, silt, or clay?

Some soil is mostly made of sand.

Soil Size

What kind of soil holds water best?

We learned that soil is made up of different things. Look at some different types of soil. You should notice that soil **particles** are different sizes. Particles are very small bits of material. They are like grains of salt.

16

Certain types of soil are better for growing plants than others. Water flows differently through soil with different sizes of particles. Some particles **absorb** more water. How does particle size affect the way water flows? Let's do an experiment to find out. We can use sand and regular soil. Sand is made of larger particles than regular soil. Start by choosing a hypothesis:

1. Water flows more quickly through soil with bigger particles.
2. Water flows more quickly through soil with smaller particles.

Let's get started!

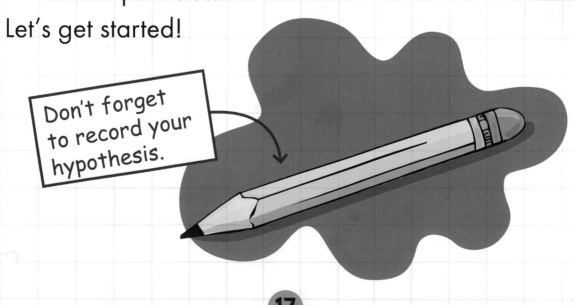

Don't forget to record your hypothesis.

Here's what you'll need:

- 1 toothpick
- 2 identical Styrofoam or paper cups, labeled Cup #1 and Cup #2
- 2 small glass jars (Each cup should fit inside the opening of each jar without falling into it.)
- 1 cup of sand
- 1 cup of soil
- 2 cups of water

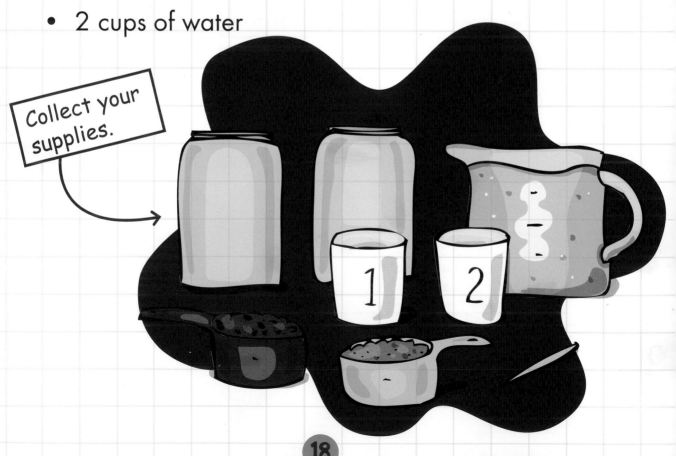

Collect your supplies.

Instructions:

1. Use the toothpick to poke 20 holes in the bottom of each cup. Space the holes evenly.
2. Place a cup in the opening of each jar.
3. Put the sand in Cup #1.

4. Put the soil in Cup #2.

5. Pour 1 cup of water into each cup.

6. Look at your jars after 1 minute. Is there liquid in either jar? Check again in 5 minutes. Write down what you see.

Conclusion:

Did you prove your hypothesis? There is little space between small soil particles. This makes it harder for water to flow through. The particles in sandy soil are larger. There are larger spaces between larger particles. This allows water to pass through the soil more quickly. Sand is not good for growing many plants. Water flows through it too quickly. Plants don't have time to absorb it.

Farm soil is good at holding water.

Stop It!

Do you think soil can work like a coffee filter?

Have you ever seen a paper **filter** in a coffeemaker? The filter holds ground coffee. Water passes through. This means no one has to worry about drinking crunchy coffee!

22

We learned that water moves more slowly through soil with smaller particles. Could soil work like a filter if the particles are small enough? Let's choose a hypothesis:

1. Soil with smaller particles can act as a filter.
2. Soil with smaller particles cannot act as a filter.

Let's get started!

Write down your hypothesis.

Here's what you'll need:

- 1 toothpick
- 1 Styrofoam or paper cup
- 1 small glass jar (The cup should fit inside the opening of the jar without falling into it.)
- 1 cup of soil (Do not use gritty soil. Liquid will pass through too quickly.)
- 1 ½ cups of prepared red Kool-Aid
- 1 clear drinking glass

Collect your supplies.

Pour 1 cup of the red drink into the soil.

Instructions:

1. Use the toothpick to poke 20 holes in the bottom of the cup. Space the holes evenly.
2. Place the cup in the opening of the jar.
3. Put the soil in the cup.
4. Pour 1 cup of the red drink into the soil.
5. Pour ½ cup of the drink into the glass.

Wait 30 to 60 minutes and then compare the liquids.

6. Wait 30 to 60 minutes. Has any liquid passed through the soil into the jar? Wait a bit longer if it hasn't.

7. Compare the liquid in the jar to the liquid in the glass. Are they the same color? Write down your observations.

Conclusion:

Was the liquid that passed through the soil a lighter color? What could that mean? Remember, smaller soil particles are closer to each other than larger ones. Some things can be trapped in the small spaces between particles. The soil filtered some of the red coloring from the water. Was your hypothesis correct?

How do your findings connect to the real world? Soil can be used in special setups to help filter dirty water.

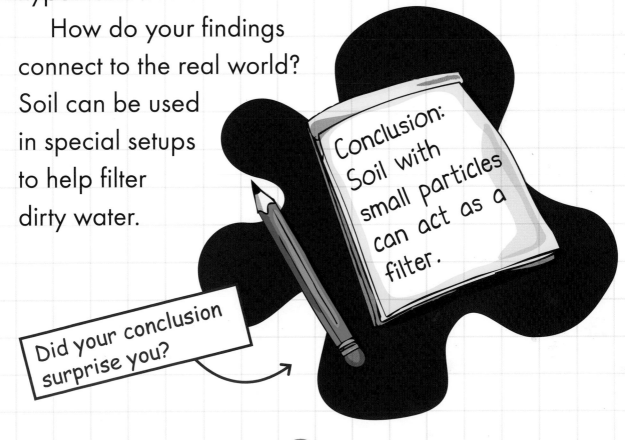

Conclusion: Soil with small particles can act as a filter.

Did your conclusion surprise you?

Do It Yourself!

Can you think of another experiment you can do with soil?

Okay, scientists! Now you know more about soil. You learned by using the scientific method. Now try thinking like a scientist to answer other questions about soil. Do plants grow bigger in different types of soil? Come up with a hypothesis. Then test it with an experiment!

What will your next experiment be?

GLOSSARY

absorb (ab-ZORB) take in

conclude (kuhn-KLOOD) to make a final decision based on what you know

conclusion (kuhn-KLOO-zhuhn) a final decision, thought, or opinion

experiment (ecks-PARE-uh-ment) a scientific way to test a guess about something

filter (FIL-tur) something that keeps certain substances from passing through

hypothesis (hy-POTH-uh-sihss) using what you know to make a guess about what will happen in an experiment

method (METH-uhd) a way of doing something

observe (uhb-ZURV) to see something or notice things by using the other senses

particles (PAR-tuh-kuhlz) very small pieces of something

silt (SILT) particles that are smaller than sand and larger than clay

textures (TEKS-churz) the feel of different materials or substances

FOR MORE INFORMATION

BOOKS

Aloian, Molly. *Different Kinds of Soil*. New York: Crabtree Publishing Company, 2009.

Korb, Rena. *Digging on Dirt*. Edina, MN: Magic Wagon, 2008.

WEB SITES

Bureau of Land Management—Just for Kids: Soil Biological Communities
www.blm.gov/nstc/soil/Kids/index.html
Learn fun facts about soil and more.

Natural Resources Conservation Service—Ask the Answer Worm!
www.nrcs.usda.gov/feature/education/squirm/skworm.html
Find answers to all of your soil questions.

INDEX

ABOUT THE AUTHOR

Vicky Franchino lives in Madison, Wisconsin, with her husband and three daughters. She now knows that soil is what you grow plants in, and dirt is what your mom makes you wash off your hands before dinner.